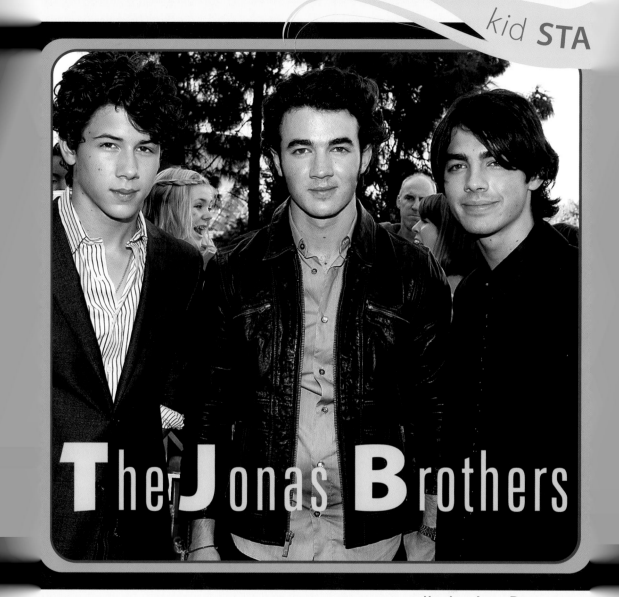

The Jonas Brothers

Katherine Rawson

PowerKiDS press.

New York

Published in 2010 by The Rosen Publishing Group, Inc.
29 East 21st Street, New York, NY 10010

First Edition

Editor: Nicole Pristash
Book Layout: Julio Gil
Photo Researcher: Jessica Gerweck

Photo Credits: Cover Kevin Winter/Getty Images; p. 4 Ethan Miller/Getty Images; p. 7 Kevin Parry/WireImage/Getty Images; pp. 8, 15 Frazer Harrison/Getty Images; pp. 11, 19 Kevin Winter/AMA/Getty Images for AMA; p. 12 Scott Gries/Getty Images; p. 16 Vince Bucci/Getty Images fo AMA; p. 20 © Mark Blinch/Reuters/Corbis.

Library of Congress Cataloging-in-Publication Data

Rawson, Katherine.
  The Jonas Brothers / Katherine Rawson. — 1st ed.
       p. cm. — (Kid stars!)
  Includes index.
  ISBN 978-1-4042-8134-9 (library binding) — ISBN 978-1-4358-3402-6 (pbk.) — ISBN 978-1-4358-3403-3 (6-pack)
  1. Jonas Brothers (Musical group)—Juvenile literature. 2. Rock musicians—United States—Biography—Juvenile literature. I. Title.
  ML3930.J62R39 2010
  782.42164092'2—dc22
  [B]
                                    2009006232

Manufactured in the United States of America

Contents

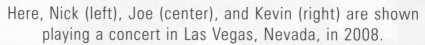

Here, Nick (left), Joe (center), and Kevin (right) are shown playing a concert in Las Vegas, Nevada, in 2008.

Meet the Jonas Brothers

Have you ever heard of the Jonas Brothers? This **popular** band plays **concerts** around the world. You may have also seen them on TV in the movie *Camp Rock*. The three members of the band are brothers. Kevin, who plays the guitar, is the oldest brother. Joe, the lead singer, is the middle brother. Nick, who also plays the guitar, is the youngest.

These talented brothers started playing music together at home when they were young. Now the Jonas Brothers are a famous band, and they have **millions** of fans. Let's find out more about their family, their music, and their plans for the **future**!

A Musical Family

The Jonas Brothers grew up in New Jersey in a **musical** family. The boys used to sing at home with their mother and father. Kevin, Joe, and Nick have a little brother, Frankie. Frankie does not play with their band, but he enjoys listening to their music.

At age six, Nick was discovered when he was singing inside a barbershop. Soon, he was singing in **Broadway** shows in New York City. Nick and his father often talked about music, and they wrote some songs together. Their Christmas song "Joy to the World" would help Nick and his brothers become famous.

The Jonas Brothers are very close to their mother, Denise (right). She often travels with the band when they play concerts.

The brothers have said that they get along very well and they almost never fight. Here they are shown playing around at the 2006 Kids' Choice Awards.

The Band Begins

Nick and his father wrote "Joy to the World" in 2002. People at a record company heard the song and liked it. They wanted Nick to make an album. In 2004, Nick's first album, *Nicholas Jonas*, was going to be **released**. However, Joe, Kevin, and Nick had written some songs together. The boys decided to form a band, and they played their music for the record company.

The record company liked their music and decided to make an album with all three brothers. *It's About Time* came out in August 2006. Few copies of the album were released, and it was not a big success.

A Big Year

The year 2007 was a big one for the Jonas Brothers. After switching record companies, the band's second album, *Jonas Brothers*, was released in August. The album went platinum. This means that more than one million copies were sold! The Jonas Brothers also played their music on the Disney Channel. After that, even more kids became fans!

On November 18, the Jonas Brothers had an **exciting** evening. They appeared at the American Music Awards. While they were **performing**, Joe fell and cut his hand, but he did not stop singing. Other singers in the music business thought the boys did a great job.

Joe, shown here, and his brothers played their song
"S.O.S." when they performed at the 2007 American Music Awards.

Here you can see the band at the first showing of *Camp Rock* in New York on June 11, 2008.

Famous Everywhere

The Jonas Brothers stayed busy in 2008. They played concerts all over the country and in Europe, too. The band even visited the White House! In June, the brothers appeared in the Disney movie *Camp Rock*. *Camp Rock* is about a young girl who goes to a music camp for kids. Joe plays Shane, one of the lead characters. Nick and Kevin play members of Joe's band, Connect 3.

In August, the band's third album, *A Little Bit Longer*, was released. More than 525,000 copies were sold in the first week! Nick wrote the **title** song. He says it is his **favorite** song to play in concert.

All About Nick

Nicholas Jerry Jonas was born on September 16, 1992, in Dallas, Texas. Nick started singing at a young age. He was around seven years old when he began singing in Broadway shows. Two of those shows were *A Christmas Carol* and *Beauty and the Beast*.

In 2005, Nick found out that he has diabetes. Diabetes is a sickness in which a person's body cannot take in sugar normally. Nick has to take **medicine** every day. It was hard at first, but he has learned how to take good care of himself. "A Little Bit Longer" is a song he wrote about having diabetes.

Nick writes many of the band's songs. He says that songwriting is his way of letting his feelings out.

Joe enjoys being onstage. He has said that even though singing can be tiring, it is worth it.

All About Joe

Joseph Adam Jonas was born on August 15, 1989, in Casa Grande, Arizona. When Joe was young, he sang at home and at church with his brothers. Singing was not his first dream, though. At first, Joe wanted to be a comedian. A comedian is a performer who tells jokes for a living. Today, Joe is the lead singer in the band. Joe likes many types of music, but rock music is his favorite.

Joe enjoys running, and he likes to play soccer. Joe has been called the loudest brother. He is very outgoing and funny, too.

All About Kevin

Paul Kevin Jonas II was born on November 5, 1987, in Teaneck, New Jersey. The "II" after his name means "the second" because Kevin has the same name as his father. Kevin is sweet and outgoing. He says he talks a lot!

When Kevin was 12 years old, he taught himself to play the guitar. Now he plays guitar and sings in the band. Kevin loves to play in front of people, and he says he is lucky to be playing music with his brothers. "We wake up every morning excited," Kevin has said, "because we get to do what we love."

Kevin sometimes sings, but he enjoys playing the guitar more. He works hard to become the best guitar player he can be.

The Jonas Brothers take time to meet their fans as much as they can. Here they are shown with some fans in Toronto, Canada, in 2008.

A Bright Future

The Jonas Brothers are busy playing concerts and appearing on TV. They even have their own movie! In February 2009, the movie *Jonas Brothers: The 3D Concert Experience* came out. The movie includes concert performances from the band's Burning Up tour in 2008. It also shows how the brothers live their lives offstage.

The most important thing to the Jonas Brothers is, of course, their music. The boys love writing songs together and sharing their music with their fans. The band plans to keep on playing for a long time. Fans can expect to hear more Jonas Brothers albums. The future looks very bright for Kevin, Joe, and Nick!

THE JONAS BROTHERS

 Although the Jonas Brothers grew up in New Jersey, they now live in Los Angeles, California.

 Kevin and Nick each own 12 guitars, and Joe owns 5.

 Nick has a dog named Elvis.

 Both Joe and Kevin like to play the board game Monopoly.

Joe is a big fan of the *High School Musical* movies.

 Joe is the tallest of the three brothers.

 Nick is a fan of the New York Yankees baseball team.

Blue is Nick's and Joe's favorite color, but Kevin's favorite is green.

History was one of Kevin's favorite subjects in school.

When he has the time, Kevin enjoys bowling.

Glossary

Broadway (BRAWD-way) A street in New York City that is famous for its theaters and the plays and musicals produced there.

concerts (KONT-serts) Public musical performances.

exciting (ik-SY-ting) Very interesting.

favorite (FAY-vuh-rut) Most liked.

future (FYOO-chur) The time that is coming.

medicine (MEH-duh-sin) A drug that a doctor gives you to help fight illness.

millions (MIL-yunz) Very large numbers.

musical (MYOO-zih-kul) Of or having to do with music.

performing (per-FORM-ing) The act of singing, dancing, acting, or playing music in front of people.

popular (PAH-pyuh-lur) Liked by lots of people.

released (ree-LEESD) Put out in stores to sell.

title (TY-tel) The name of a song, book, album, painting, or other work.

Index

A

album(s), 9–10, 13, 21

C

Camp Rock, 5, 13
concerts, 5, 13, 21

E

evening, 10

G

guitar(s), 5, 18, 22

J

Jonas, Joe, 5–6, 9–10, 13, 17, 21–22
Jonas, Kevin, 5–6, 9, 13, 18, 21–22
Jonas, Nick, 5–6, 9, 13–14, 21–22

N

New Jersey, 6, 18, 22

S

singer(s), 5, 10, 17
song(s), 6, 9, 13–14, 21

T

TV, 5, 21

Web Sites

Due to the changing nature of Internet links, PowerKids Press has developed an online list of Web sites related to the subject of this book. This site is updated regularly. Please use this link to access the list:
www.powerkidslinks.com/kids/jonas/